Sixpence in My Shoe

Best Wishes
Maureen Mason
January 2009.

By

Maureen Mason

authorHOUSE®

AuthorHouse™ UK Ltd.
500 Avebury Boulevard
Central Milton Keynes, MK9 2BE
www.authorhouse.co.uk
Phone: 08001974150

First published by AuthorHouse 6/30/2008

ISBN: 978-1-4343-8895-7 (sc)

Printed in the United States of America
Bloomington, Indiana

This book is printed on acid-free paper.

Foreword

Most people look back on their school days with mixed emotions, and I am no exception. However, I well remember a time when I was about eight or nine and still a junior at Castleton Primary School in Armley, Leeds.

We were a class of forty-eight children, and our teacher at that time was one Miss Topham. She was fifty if she was a day, and had short grey bobbed hair and steely blue eyes to match. It was a case of, woe betide anyone who brought about her displeasure!

She was the strictest disciplinarian I have ever come across in the whole of my life, and the fairest. She firmly believed that good behaviour should be rewarded, and liked nothing better than to perch on her high stool and (quote) "indulge the class" (unquote.) from her wealth of stories and poetry.

To this day I can remember word for word, almost all of the poems that she used to recite to us, *William the Conqueror*, *Mustard and Cress*, and *Latitude and Longitude* were just a few. Her most favourite poem, and one that never failed to bring a tear to her eye was a beautiful one, and I have never been able to discover the name of its author.

The first line goes like this: - A pure white mantle blotted out the world I used to know -

"Biddy" as she was unofficially known to the class, had been engaged to be married at the outbreak of the First World War but her Fiancé was killed in action in France. She never married, and never became a Mother, save to those children she taught like me.

The love of poetry and story writing that was born in me at that time has stayed with me always, and I shall never cease to be grateful for the legacy that she left behind when she touched our lives all those years ago.

If you are looking to regain your lost childhood, I hope that this is the kind of memory that you are looking for, it is certainly one that I shall never forget.

Dedicated with love and affection
to my late husband Stanley.
My daughters Linda and Elaine
and to my grandsons
Adam, Matthew and Robert.

CONTENTS

Sixpence In My Shoe

Today it is your wedding day.
When you walk down the aisle,
you'll have a sixpence in your shoe
please walk on it with style.

If you walk on silver
as you become a bride,
then poverty and hard times
are never by your side.

It's just a superstition
or so I've heard it said.
and now I pass it on to you
on the day that you are wed.

AMBITION

One day when I become full –grown,
a writer I shall be.
Every word will be my own,
and the Queen shall come to tea.

I'll show her all the work I've done,
and all the prizes I have won.
and when I'm an expert she'll ask me,
to write down her biography.

THE CITY OF LEEDS

The Town Hall at the centre of the city,
the Civic Hall and the University.
The Post Office Buildings, Queens Hotel,
and Black Prince stands in the Square as well.
The Corn Exchange and Victoria Quarter,
Granary Wharf right next to the water.

Woodhouse Lane with the B.B.C.
Kirkstall Road and Yorkshire T.V.
Temple Newsam and Lotherton Hall,
Roundhay Park, we have them all.
The City Varieties, The Playhouse, The Grand
no finer theatres in all the land.
Shall I go on? I've sown all the seeds,
surely you've guessed, my home town is Leeds

Love?

Let me snuggle down with you,
feel the warmth of your arms around me.
The warm, and soft, gentle touch of you,
against my skin.
Your welcome, at my approach
is always there.
My warm and cosy,
comfy armchair!

ARMLEY FOLK

I was born in Thornton Place,
that's just off Armley road.
Where everyone knew every face,
and some were quite outspoken.

We kids all went to Castleton,
that was the local school.
To read and write and do our sums,
that was the golden rule.

We used to spend our evenings
sitting on the railway wall,
watching the "Flying Scot" go by
the door of Armley Hall.

Friday night was always
bath night I recall.
with a fire beneath the old set pot,
and the tin bath from off the wall.
Dad always went to the local pub,
Mum, and the kids went in the tub.
The youngest first, then the next,
and so on right to Mum.

Then we would sit and listen to the radio,
intent on what was being said.
Dad usually came in around nine-o clock
to make sure that we all went to bed

Our New Home

I never thought we'd leave the house
we'd shared for all those years.
A place that gave us shelter
through our laughter and our tears.
until we found our bungalow,
A place exceeding small.
Looking so dejected and uncared for,
I recall.

With this bungalow we've had
an instant love affair.
The whole place has blossomed,
with our tender loving care.
There is a wealth of happiness
that cannot be denied,
when we close our new front door
and leave the world outside.

LOVING FRIENDS

We met in love,
in that same love we were both torn apart.
The years have passed
and with their passing healed the pain,
yet time has not dimmed my belief
that we shall meet again.
Today I saw you quite by chance,
you did not know nor did you even glance
and as I looked once more upon your face,
my heart leaped my pulse began to race.
The magic is still there; we have not reached the end
there is still time for us, to call each other friend.

AUTUMN LOVE

When we were young and in our teens,
you were the Hero who haunted my dreams.
The man who chose me to share his life,
my only wish was to be your wife.

Together we scaled such dizzy heights,
with passionate days, and ecstatic nights.
Magic times full of laughter and love,
those were the days of our summertime love.

The days which turned into years, have flown,
your life has ended, and I live alone.
Now, a new man is a part of my life.
One day soon I shall be his wife.

Our wants and needs are different now,
he takes the time to show me how
romance can be savoured, like a good wine.
To be lingered over, and matured with time.

Though we have reached our autumn years,
still there is laughter, and sometimes tears.
Something new to discover each day,
sharing together, our work and our play.

We know that our days will grow shorter each year,
but we can be sure there is nothing to fear.
While we have each other, and God's up above,
we'll share in the glory of our autumn love.

Price Above Rubies

We can't afford the rubies
to celebrate our Forty years.
Our children are our jewels,
and the children that are theirs.

So accept this dozen roses,
of course they are ruby red.
To celebrate these forty years,
of loving you instead.

SENIOR CITIZEN

I've just been for my Twirly,
there was no delay.
It's valid 'til 2000,
and I can use it right away.

Whenever I go shopping
between nine thirty and three,
Because I am a Pensioner
my Bus Pass goes with me.

And now that I've turned sixty
it seems I must retire,
I've time to do so many things,
whatever I desire.

I go out bright and early
not one to make a fuss
just ask "Am I too early for my Pass?"
As I step on the bus.

Travelling by bus or train
is of no consequence to me
I can journey almost anywhere
as long as I'm back by three!

Friends And Neighbours.

For years we lived across the street,
on occasion we would meet.
We'd stop and smile and say "Hello"
then on our journey we would go.

We never had too much to say
until the day we moved away.
"Goodbye, good luck", and,
"Don't forget keep in touch."
The kind of thing Folks always say
I guess we said it all that day.

One day the 'phone began to ring
"I wondered if you'd settled in?"
that conversation I recall
was the beginning of it all.

By letter and by telephone
we have kept in touch,
the friendship that has blossomed
has come to mean so much.

It seems to me it's such a crime
that we have wasted so much time.
The question now each time we meet,
"Why weren't we friends when we lived
on the street?"

GRANDPA'S GARDEN.

In my Grandpa's garden
such lovely flowers grow.
There's fruit and veg
and chickens legs,
for dinner when we go.

In my Grandpa's garden
It's a lovely place to be.
There's always something to be done,
but there's always time for me.

In my Grandpa's garden
such lovely flowers grow,
and often people passing by
just stop to say "Hello."

And when it's time for us to leave,
he takes us in his car.
And then he comes back home again,
to where the flowers are.

Fantasy Island.

Shipwrecked Mariners were we three,
though we never left our own front room.
Sailing the world in a clipped rug ship
my Brother, Sister and me.

With a fireguard sail on a cold stone sea,
and the family cat for a crew.
We'd sail round the world
and be back before tea,
My Brother, Sister and me.

In furniture forests lions and tigers lurked,
shipwrecked Mariners we.
With chicken claw soup and dripping and bread,
my Brother, Sister and me.

It's a good fifty years since we travelled abroad,
but we're still here to tell you this tale
thank the Lord.
my Brother, Sister and me.

MOTHER

Farewell to you my darling Mum,
the eternal sleep for you has not yet come.
Though you have wandered far away from me,
far into the mists of yesterday.

No longer now can you recall my name,
or the best beloved child that I became.
The happy times, the joys we shared,
whilst growing up I always knew you cared.

The look of childlike trust I see upon your face,
as I take your hand and lead you gently to
another place.
It might only be into the room next door
and yet you don't remember being there
before.

Dear Pal of mine what shall I do,
when the eternal sleep at last
takes hold of you?
and leads you gently by the hand,
to all your loved ones in that promised land.

You don't look back, nor do you hesitate,
I see you standing there at Heavens gate.
Now I am left with grief and tears,
and the beautiful memories of our special years.

The years roll by and I no longer can recall
your face,
I wonder are you happy in that other place?
I fancy that you watch me from above,
enfolding me in your eternal love.

The Writing Lesson.

My Father taught me how to write,
to set down the words and form them just right.
First the A and then the B,
it was never easy for me.

He penned the words with fluid grace,
my first attempts were all over the place.
Write the up strokes thin, and the thick strokes down
just the way that you are shown.

He taught me how to use the pen,
with infinite patience again and again.
He set down the words upon the page,
and never once flew in a rage.

My Dad has long since left this life,
left behind this world of strife.
But a wonderful legacy he left me,
when he taught me to write my ABC.

Quiz Night

Every Sunday we take part in a quiz,
how, where, why, who is?
Who will help us in our plight
will we ever get things right?

Are our minds complete blanks
or are we just as thick as planks?
Entering into a weekly quiz,
when we none of us know what day this is.

The questions number one to twenty,
believe me folks, that's more than plenty.
The first one's right, now six and seven.
guess what folks; we've scored eleven!

DAYDREAMS

In my minds eye I can see
all those things I should like to be.
Opera singer, Olympic swimmer,
even a football pools winner.

Cyclist, hypnotist
even a philatelist.
And if I should be so bold,
I'll try my hand at mining gold.

Astronaut, juggernaut,
fashionable lady sipping port.
A trapeze artist flying high,
all these am I in my minds eye

THE OLD ARMCHAIR.

There's nothing quite like a cosy armchair,
the place to relax and forget all your care.
Beautifully built to accommodate one,
the place to relax when your day's work is done.

Just close your eyes and sit back with ease,
catnap or daydream just as you please.
Free to imagine whatever you dare,
in the fantasy world of your cosy armchair.

A
Yorkshire Lass
And A Bus Pass

Ah've bin to get me Twirly
an' they'v e gein me this 'ere pass.
Na ah doan't naw what thev done it fer,
'cos ahm nobbut just a Lass.
I reckon it'll coom in 'andy though,
when ah can think on summat forrit.
Until 't fust time ah gets on 't bus,
an' finds that ah've fergorrit!

In Despair

Deep within the height of me,
the width, the breadth, the soul of me.
I ache for life, the way it used to be.
When you still lived, and breathed,
and loved with me

I sit and look at your vacant chair,
and in my mind I find you sitting there.
I see you through a mist of tears,
and I thank God for all the happy years

The days are long, and lonely now.
my nights are cavernous, and empty now.
I wonder where you are, if you can see,
this deep despair, that's fast engulfing me.

Your voice, your presence, and your touch
your quick concern, your tenderness, I miss so much.
The look of love forever on your face,
even in death, could never be replaced.

THE LEARNING CURVE

When I set out on the learning curve
I was only three,
That was when I first began
to learn my ABC.

Twelve years later I left school;
no learning for a while,
But reading Writing and 'Rithmetic
I'd learned them all with style.

I never got a scholarship,
Degree or GCE's,
Yet knitting, sewing, cooking,
I'd learned them all with ease.

I learned how to be a daughter,
and get on with my life,
Lo, and behold, before too long
I learned to be a wife.

Next I became a Mother,
and everything was new.
Then I became a Grandma,
I had some help there too.

Sixty years have come and gone
and now I'm back at school.
Studying computers is the golden rule.

You have to keep up with the times,
or so I have been told,
Learning is the only thing
that stops you growing old.

So I turn up every Friday,
and do my bit you see,
To keep up with our youngsters,
even though I'm sixty-three!

Spare Time

What is it that kids have in common these days?
lots of spare time.
No jobs - no homes - no place to go
boredom is a killer – and spare time.
What to do for pleasure – time for leisure,
lots of spare time.

Hang out in bars – steal a few cars,
thieving's all the rage, in their spare time.
Carrying guns – chicken runs,
anything for kicks in their spare time.
Brave young thugs, some even do drugs.

What they really need is - love
and some of our spare time.
They need to work no need to shirk,
you can have their cardboard houses
and their spare time.

Free Time

What do you do with your free time?
I asked myself today.
How do you while away the hours
when you have time to play?
That cardigan you had to knit
that surely wouldn't wait.
And what about those fancy cakes
you like to decorate?
The poetry that you set down
whenever you have time.
The frustration that you always feel
when the words just will not rhyme.
I guess with all the many things
you really like to do,
Free time is only ever there
for other folks not you.

Holiday Island

It's wonderful here,
the weather is clear.
But it's so hard to think
about slimming,
I'll try to be good,
do the things that I should
And certainly do lots of swimming.

Then when I get back,
I'll get straight back on track
work at it with
heart and with soul.
Then maybe one day,
I'll be able to say
that I finally made it to GOAL!

MEMORIES OF A LOST LOVE

I wander through the avenues of my mind
and once again discover thoughts of you.
Of how you'd hesitate each time we met,
yet at the same time hurry to my side.

Your pride, the day you took me as your bride.
Tenderly I gather up the fragments of your kisses,
and hold them gently to me for all time.
For surely it was you, who taught me -
that's what bliss is.

I walk along the pathway of my memories,
remembering the joys we shared,
just talking to each other.
And the delight in our discoveries.

The years have passed and still,
your love is reaching out to me.
Far beyond the doorway to eternity,
that you walked through.
Leaving me behind -to remember.

THE WAYWARD LAD

"I'll never make that bus now" said John,
hastily pulling his trousers on.
He'd spent the time looking round the town
wondering where his son had gone.

He'd left the house just the night before
vowing he'd never come back any more.
There'd been a row about using drugs
John said users are just mugs.

He couldn't believe the lad had left home,
There was no telling where he'd gone
He heard a knock at his front door
"That'll be the Police for sure."

"He shouldn't have gone off in a huff,
I'll bet he spent the night sleeping rough.
Yet in spite of all the pain,
I'll be glad to see him home again."

Shamefaced the lad stood there at the door,
"Dad, can we try again once more?"
"Come on in Lad", his voice was gruff.
"I never meant to be so tough".

"Your Mum and I always live in hope,
that you'll have the sense to keep off dope.
Where have you been all night anyhow?
I'm never going to make that bus now"

I Wonder

I wonder what the roads are like up in the skies,
where the aeroplane flies?
and do the angels hitch hike
across the galaxy!

Once they are settled in their berth,
are they reluctant to come down to earth?
When they arrive at their location,
in some exotic destination?

Would they land upon the moon?
if they took a flight in the month of June!
or if their freight were motor cars,
would they journey on the highway to the stars?

This not the way it is you see,
they book their seats like you and me,
doing their travelling twenty four seven,
living their lives in seventh heaven!

WHEN I WAS YOUNG

I loved my roots, the cobbled streets,
where back to backs and pavements meet.
Tall black chimneys belching smoke,
tower above the working folk.

The weavers in their torn black pinnies,
the mill hands, and the spinning Jennie's.
They say the world's a better place,
the landscape has a whole new face.

In this world of hustle and bustle,
no one ever hears the rustle
of silken skirts as she passes by,
the Ghost of happier days gone by.

I know they never can come back,
but folks today don't have the knack,
of learning the best way to cope,
when times are hard and they lack hope.

In days gone by those cobbled streets
rang with the echoes of neighbours' feet.
Ready to don their hats and coats
and lend a hand to other folks.

The council hadn't driven in the wedges
like garden gates and privet hedges.
Folks nowadays don't like to interfere,
I wonder do they know we're living here?

There's violence, and guns, and hate,
yet we call each other Mate,
when things go wrong then "It's not fair."
Who will admit –they just don't care.

Now we have those who shoot up drugs
folks who don't then they're just Mugs,
Why don't we legalise the drugs as well,
and pave the way to "Merry Hell"?

What Is A Parent?

Parents are two very special people,
whether or not they are naturally your own,
or a couple you just happened to adopt along the way.
Parents are people, who will love you all your life,
whether you deserve it or not.

They will stand by you in times of trouble
and praise you to the heavens
when you have done something good.
Parents are only human, they shout and get mad,
when they think you've been bad.
But go on loving you just the same.

Parents are the folk who
teach you right from wrong.
Who amuse you when you're bored,
can make you laugh without a word.

Parents are the people you can go to
when no one else wants to know
and be glad, just because you're there.
Most of all Parents are
exactly what you have made them,
just by being born.

They will tell you with a smile
that every minute has been worthwhile,
each time you say
in your own special way,
"Hello Mum, hello Dad"

My Daughters

My Daughters you will never know
how dear you are to me,
From the day that you were born
you've brought such joy to me.

Every day I watched you grow
with such love and special pride
and then one day you walked away
with a young man by your side.

Before too long you gave to me
three grandsons that I adore,
and my heart just swells with pride.
Never has there been a home
with any more love inside.

And when at last my time is come,
as it surely must
my love for you will carry on
when I have turned to dust.

The Widow

A New Year, a new life.
now a Widow, no longer a wife.
Where to go, what to do
the rest of your life in front of you.
At last you're coming through the pain
of learning to live alone again.
Set out to do the best you can,
if not for yourself, then do it for your Man

Back To Basics

Let's get back to basics
whatever that phrase means.
Let's put truth and honesty
back upon the scene.

Cut out all the packaging
the glitz and all the frills.
And see life as it really is
with all its pain and ills.

It's time for some plain speaking
let's call a spade a spade.
Call in some past favours
keep those promises we made.

Cultivate integrity honesty and truth
instil some sense of purpose
into our wayward youth.

Have we no compassion
for our homeless waifs and strays.
For those who share the hardships
that fills their lonely days?

If we hold out a helping hand
to soothe away their strife.
And give the poor and needy
a brand new start in life.

We can hold our heads up high
we shall not need to hide.
We can rebuild our Nation
and restore its shattered pride.

If we get back to basics
before it is too late.
Then we shall have found the key
that made Great Britain - Great.

The Victim

Alarm bells are ringing
look out is the coast clear?
Shove that video in the van
and let's get out of here.

Look out someone's coming
it's better if we go.
One vicious knock upon the head
that's the last thing he'll ever know

What' the use of being honest
what's the use of being right.
If we can't help the other guy
without being in a fight.

What is wrong with this old world
if we can't tell right from wrong?
Let's stop this endless thieving
and leave things where they belong.

THE GIFT

There is something in all of us
exquisitely designed,
That is only used by some of us
and only when inclined.

It has no bounds nor limits
unaware of time or space.
Has access to the infinite
and needs no resting place.

It does not need our bodies
to do its endless task.
And will always find an answer
to anything we ask.

It can make our thoughts accessible
to our loved ones far and near.
And turn into reality
those dreams we hold most dear.

It can make all things possible
which is why it was designed.
Gods gift to every one of us
this wonderous thing, the mind

Conversation

There is an air of sanity
about the world when you're with me.
And time appears of no account,
at least it never does amount
to anything when you are there.
We have so much to say and share
it passes by on silent wings,
while we're discussing other things
that most folks find uninteresting.

We shall not put the world to rights
in maybe half a dozen nights.
Yet in our minds we can create
a world that's free from fear and hate.
That we may enter hand in hand
a place that can be wonderland.
Filled with wonder and elation
because, we had our conversation.

OUR GRANDCHILDREN

May I introduce our Grandchildren
ages four and five.
Both so very special
and very much alive.

Adam James, the elder
blond haired with eyes of blue.
Full of fun and mischief
but very loving too.

Matthew Alan, he came after
he can fill your days with laughter.
They turn the grey skies into blue
when they say "Grandma we love you!"

Robert Andrew, the youngest one,
is just as loving, and just as much fun
So full of mischief it has to be said.
from rising each morning, 'til going to bed.

Now Robert he is not yet three,
he came much later on you see.
Big brother Matthew now is ten
he plays football with a boy called Ben.

We look forward to their visits
such fun we have, and then
There's always something new to do
when they come round again.

Childhood

I recall when I was small
Mother's eyes, and the way that she smiled.
When I looked at the world
through the eyes of a child

I remember when I was three
seeing my very first Christmas tree.
It seemed to be ten foot taller than me
but then I was only small you see.

The magic of a bouncing ball
of daddy's footsteps in the hall.
Nursery rhyme pictures on the wall
These are the things that I recall.

Happy hours playing in the sun
ice cream and candy- floss just for fun.
Building sand castles by the sea
and scurrying home in time for tea.

Kittens tangled in a skein of wool
rosy red apples round and full.
Witches fairies and goblins too
shadows that sometimes frightened you.

Snowflakes falling on the ground
the magic of wintertime all around.
Melting swiftly if they should land
into the palm of a warm little hand

Then at night jumping into bed
being tucked in and prayers being said.
Bedtime stories and angels who keep
watch over me when I'm fast asleep.

LONELINESS

I know that I am not in love with you
yet there is one thing that I would ask of you.
Can you explain to me and to my satisfaction
just what it is the source of this attraction.
That draws me without hesitation to your side
unerring as a willing bride.

I feel a need for you I will admit
though sexual attraction is no part of it.
Why do I miss you more and more?
Each time you leave and walk out of the door
as though each thought I've saved a million years.
Needs to be poured into your hearing ears
words that I have uttered in the past,
fell on deaf ears and were not meant to last.

Folks never meant to be unkind
they did not hear what was within my mind.
Why then this reluctance when I know the score
to stand alone the way I did before?
Maybe I just can't stand the pain
of facing life alone again.

HOME 2000

Millennium dome,
sterile home, with lots of chrome.
Robotic dogs, all wheels and cogs
automatic showers, sprinkle the flowers.
Solar heating takes some beating.
all done by remote, does it get your vote,
What a life, who needs a wife?

Memories

Life is tranquil and serene
memories are evergreen
Skies above are ever blue
whenever I remember you

I remember sunny days
followed by autumns misty haze.
Warm cosy evenings in the firelight glow
crisp frosty mornings and winter snow.

New- born lambs a crisp new day
laughing children with time to play.
Summers last rose soft kissed with dew
all these are wrapped in memories of you.

THE PEOPLE'S PRINCESS.

There's a bright new star
in the heavens tonight.
Just to the right of the moon
I wonder could it be Diana?
a life that was ended too soon.

We had no way of knowing
the way that the world would behave.
All the tears the grief and the flowers
for a life that no one could save.

How will the world fare without her?
it's too painful to hazard a guess.
I'm sure she will not be forgotten
she's Diana the people's princess

The Circle Of Life

The eternal mother rests her hands
upon the belly of the pregnant earth
and feels the gentle stirrings of her unborn young.
Eager anticipation spurs on the imminent birth.
A warm and gentle glow envelops all the earth
young buds burst on tree and stem
and the birds sing clear.
Mother Nature smiles well pleased
at last the spring is here.

This child has reached the summer of her youth
learned well the mysteries of wisdom and of truth.
Loved by the world who adores her warmth and
splendour,
Born to be his she gives herself to him in sweet
surrender.
Earth mother looks upon her child with pride
how beautiful she is this summer bride.

The world and his wife are dressed in autumn glory now
the fruits of their union bend low every bough.
The white haired mother nods approval to her son
knowing that her task in life is almost done.
Aware that when she treads the earth no more
life will go on just as it did before.

Swiftly now the winter of her life draws nigh
the trees and blossoms of her early youth
stand stark and bare against the cold night sky.
Beneath the earth she begins her long nights sleep
still as death her vigil she will keep
Cared for through the bitter cold and rain
'til spring- time comes and she's reborn again.

THE LIBRARY

The year is nineteen thirty nine
Crossgates lads are on the front line.
Yet life goes on much the same,
survival is the name of the game.

Mums are out at work each day
the kids go out in the streets to play.
Yet there is danger all around,
each of us listening for the siren sound.

Crossgates just isn't the same any more,
now that our lads have gone to war.
Fathers, husbands, sons and brothers,
nowt but anguish for wives and mothers.

Some say that it's nowt but a phoney war,
makes you wonder what the fighting's for.
There's a battle going on up the river Plate
our new library opened on the very same date.

We have the black-out, we have to stay home,
it's just unsafe the streets to roam.
I went up to the library just for a look,
and came back home with a real good book

The old place was in Austhorpe road you know,
the new ones better, more of a show.
Plenty to choose from when it comes to the books
but it's about what you can learn, not how it looks.

Most women are working up at Barnbow
Tthe ordnance factory don't you know.
They are responsible for building the tanks
but the wages they pay won't break any banks.

At least the kids have a place for their learning
their knowledge must improve their earning.
Now they can also read for pleasure,
something new to do with their leisure.

When at last this war is done
and our menfolk have come home.
Then at last the tide will turn
and we shall all have time to learn.

The Phantom Lady

I gaze across the rolling lawns and see
a stately home that seems to say to me,
"Come inside and look around
at all these treasures I have found.
Collected from a bygone age
the evidence of our heritage."

Housed within these stately halls
tapestries hang upon the walls.
Whilst portraits silver and polished oak
visions of the past evoke.
Where marble busts and statues stand
fashioned by the craftsman's hand.

Now in my garden lovers meet
unaware of ghostly feet
that travel to the temple where
I the lady Isobel wait there.
For even though my love has gone
I shall remain 'til he comes home.

On moonlit nights I walk beside the lake
knowing that if only for his sake,
I shall roam across this land
until he takes me by the hand
and when he draws me to his breast.
Only then shall I find eternal rest

THE "CATS EYES" MAN

When travelling on the motorway
do we ever stop to say
A quiet thank you to the man,
who gave a thought to each car and van
that travels on our roads today,
as we journey on our way?

Do we ever stop to think
how every single glassy wink,
guides us through the fog and rain
and leads us safely home again,
As we travel through the night
on roads without a single light.

When you are driving in the dark
you can see those studs that mark
the centre of the road for us,
and on these your eyes will focus
as the darkened roads you scan.
Remember him he's the "cats eyes" man.

Dedicated to the memory of Percy Shaw. The man
who invented the "cats eyes" road safety system

GRANDPA

Our Grandpa has a new garden
it's up in Heaven above.
He likes to tend it every day
for all those that we love.
He left behind a special place
where Grandma lives alone.
With lots of happy memories
and each and every one
are all about our Grandpa,
and the way he lived his life
and our Grandma knew him best of all,
because she was his wife.

LOVE IS:-

Love is a memory of you
being always at my side.
A memory of the day
you took me as your bride.

A memory of a touch
that made me flutter like a bird.
A memory of eyes
that filled with laughter at a word.

A memory that you
will always care for me.
A memory that
our love will always be.

A memory that
when we reach the end.
You will be there
to welcome me, my friend.

GOODBYE

It's always hard to say goodbye
hold up your head, try not to cry.
To learn to live again alone
hold up your head and carry on.

To bear the heartache and the pain
and find the laughter in the rain.
Then all at once the sun breaks through
and suddenly you're glad you're you.

TWICE THE VALUE

Twice the value and only half the fat
that's me the weight watcher
what do you think of that?
I've counted points and calories
lost inches here and there.
Now I can even stand with ease
when I get up from my chair.
I've said "no" to sweets and chocolates
and "can you eat this last bread roll?"
I will say "No" to anything
if it helps me reach my goal.
I've been to all the dress shops
tried some "fat Frocks" and some "Thin."
And now I know which pair of shoes
I like best being in.
So if you want to be a winner
and lose a stone or three,
Then come along to "weight watchers"
and be a "loser" just like me

A PROPER GENT

Once there lived a warm and gentle man
all those who knew him called him Stan.
An animal lover and a gardener was he
who lived for his wife and his family.

She was a teenager, when he met his wife
for forty odd years she shared his life.
They had their ups and downs it's true
just as thousands of others do.

Then their two daughters came along
changing their lives from a rhyme to a song.
He worked very hard it has to be said
providing food and shelter and a roof over their heads.

Until the time when their children were grown
gone out in the world made homes of their own.
Then their three grandchildren came along
filling their lives once again with a song.

Now the story has changed for Stanley has gone
back home to his Maker leaving Maureen alone,
In their home there is lots of sadness it's true
but there is a host of happy memories too.

As she sits there alone and reflects on their life
Maureen's glad she agreed to become his wife.
For although there were folks who said, "they're too young"
she was happy and proud to be his number one.

If You Remember

If you remember to forget me
as I walk away from you.
And remember to forget the time
I fell in love with you.
Remember to forget the little things
we've said and done.
Remember to forget the time
you said your mine alone.
If you remember to forget me
as you leave to catch your train.
Then perhaps you will remember
to forget to feel the pain.
But if you remember to forget
last night you said we're through.
Then Darling I'll remember
just to keep on loving you.

Kosovo

These children of Kosovo, so full of despair,
have lost all their loved ones, doesn't anyone care.
Bewildered and frightened, standing alone
isn't there someone to give them a home?

Eyes full of sadness devoid of all hope
how do we expect these infants to cope?
The evil that lurks in our world today
the fight for supremacy, some one must pay.

At the end of the day what is it all for?
it's high time we ended this lust for war.
The death and the carnage no man should see
especially babies of one, two and three!

A Virgin Mind

A virgin mind, this was my gift to you,
there to be tilled the way that farmers do.
The seeds of thought you planted there for me
were set with care, the way they ought to be.
And fed on tears that I shed in the past
for all the golden hours that could not last.
They have been sown in rich good earth
and now are heralding the birth
of a rich full harvest yet to be.
To match the mind that first you showed to me.

All In A Days Work

Sitting in my office chair
I wonder what I'm doing there.
Adding figures all day long
this is not where I belong.

Answering the telephone, personal address
again the 'phone is ringing
"Hello, good morning, yes.
Typing, filing wages to be done
workaday morning's scarce begun.

Invoices, costings, ghastly VAT.
no time for daydreams about that cup of tea.
Parcels, telegrams, letters to be sent
I swear, when I retire, I'll go live in a tent!

Poor Ethel

Have you ever met Mrs Ethel?
she's the Mum of my Daughter's best friend.
A really good sort Mrs Ethel,
on her you can surely depend.
That's Ethel!

While at the supermarket one morning
making sure that their prices were right,
She was standing there at the checkout
when down on her head dropped a light
Poor Ethel!

They picked her up off the ground
and when she came round,
she'd a whacking great lump on her head.
"Now come along Dear, we can't leave you here,
You could wake up and find yourself dead!"
Poor Ethel!

She will tell you she's not a great scholar,
who knows, maybe she's right.
She could be an overnight genius,
now she's finally seen the light.
Poor Ethel!

Valentine

Who always hears every word that I've said,
who always keeps my feet warm in bed
Who never leaves me on my own,
after everyone else has gone.
Who always shoots the biggest line?
only you my VALENTINE.

THE FINAL COUNTDOWN

The final countdown has begun
't is the eve of the millennium.
A brand new century a bright new age
what will be written on this brand new page?

Shall we find new ways to fight disease?
or create new lottery winners to live lives of ease.
Will we fly to Jupiter set foot on Mars
and increase the taxes on our brand new cars?

Will we teach our children to want more and more
take from the rich to give to the poor?
It doesn't have to be this way
this is the start of a brand new day

Let us make a brand new start
listen to our heart of hearts.
And as this bright new day unfolds
don't make the same mistakes of old.

We can create a world of peace
where war and conflict at last will cease.
These are the best gifts that we can give
to the world where our children have to live.

Now that all the seeds are sown
and our old fashioned ways have been outgrown
make this a new world all our own,
Before the final countdown.

Una & Alwyn Dunn

This is a story I'd like to tell,
of a couple I once knew very well.
He, was a Yorkshireman, she came from Devon,
theirs was a marriage made in heaven.
There were no children to bless their life,
they lived for each other, husband and wife.
Yet there was always laughter and plenty of fun,
in the lives of Una & Alwyn Dunn.

They met at the start of the Second World War,
freedom and justice is what they fought for.
They fought in the battles side by side,
'til finally Una became Alwyn's bride.
Then home to Yorkshire he finally brought her,
for the family to meet its newest daughter.
Their life together at last begun,
for Mr & Mrs Alwyn Dunn.

After the war Alwyn went down the pit,
the work was hard, but it kept him fit.
Una worked in a factory, though that wasn't the plan
in the course of their work, that was how it began,
The best of friendships, with Maureen & Stan.
There was always laughter and lots of fun,
to be found with Una & Alwyn Dunn.

Alwyn's garden was his pride and joy
he loved the soil from being a boy.
Una shared his hobby too,
for those two practically anything grew.
In fact they were known for miles around,
for the plants that they grew in Gods good ground.
They were two of the best, you can ask anyone
this couple called Una & Alwyn Dunn

Now it is sad, but their lives have ended,
gone is the home and the garden they tended.
At last they're together, and not down hearted,
happy now that they're reunited.
There's surely a garden in Heaven above,
for them to nurture and love.
I'll always remember the laughter, the fun,
that we shared with Una & Alwyn Dunn.

What's A Poppy Dad?

What is a poppy Dad? asked the young lad
The older man looked at his son and said
these are the flowers that grew in the field
where the young men lay dead
red as the blood those young soldiers shed.

It's centre is as black as the horror of war
and everyone vowed there would be no more.
There are millions of poppies on the battlefields
blood red are the petals that fall like the dead.
What is a poppy the young lad said?

The poppy's an emblem, a symbol you see,
there to remind folks, just like you and me.
Because of these wars and the blood that was shed
the likes of us can sleep sound in our beds
that is the poppy, the flower of the dead.

Summertime

Once again it's summertime,
the earth is cracked and dry.
Yet all the while the sun shines down,
relentlessly from the sky.

Our trees and plants are shrivelled,
the earth has turned to dust.
On and on this drought goes on
and we begin to thirst for water

The gentle healing rain
to fill our lakes and rivers,
Turn the whole world green again
our water is so precious we must not act in haste
Don't turn those taps and hosepipes on
and let it run to waste

LIFE IS A SONG.

We met on an Island In The Sun,
our Summer Holiday, scarce begun.
Here It Comes Again, That Loving Feeling.
that has me Dancing On The Ceiling.

We were two Strangers On The Shore,
Day By Day, I love you More.
I Believe, Night And Day,
You'll Be Mine, If I Had My Way.

You Are The Sunshine Of My Life,
if you'll consent to be my wife,
I Will Love You, As I've Loved You,
all my life!

At Last, I'm back in my Home Town,
with my little Alice Blue Gown.
Folks keep saying we're Too Young
but that's just another song waiting to be sung.

To Norman

Norman, dear and gentle man
we miss you so.
Are you re-united with your darling Lily
is that why you had to go?

Did she call your name
and draw you gently to her side?
What were you feeling
as you crossed that great divide?

That night you held so tightly to my hand,
until at last she came and led you gently
To that promised land.
Into that place that's free from pain and tears
an end to all the suffering in your eight and eighty years.

While we are left to mourn and celebrate your life
you at last, are re-united with your wife
Sleep well Norman, you have earned your rest
to us dear Uncle you were the best.

Soulmates

What is this wonderful instrument the mind
if the body; which contains it, must be left behind?
When Lovers only in space can meet,
and not on earth, in just an ordinary street.

What then the fate of these two human hearts
if the bodies which contain them must be kept apart?
What of this love, if these same bodies are ignored
will it survive on food for thought and be restored?

If their next life must be another time, another place.
will this love know this other being, this new face?
And remember this now, which will be their past,
when they first declared this love they vowed would last.

SUMMER LOVE

Golden sands and a twinkling star
swaying palms over one parked car,
A perfect setting for a wonderful night of love.
Now my Darling here we are
a lovers moon and one parked car,
Kiss me my sweet 'til my heart beats like a drum.
Hold me tightly to your heart, tell me we shall never part.

I always knew that I would find someone,
now we dream of the day we shall be one.
There will be golden sands and summer skies
and heaven shining in your eyes.
Salty breezes that softly croon
through swaying palms to a lovers moon,
shining softly down over one parked car.

My Valentine

It's many years since first we met,
and you have always been my girl.
Through the years it's grown better yet,
and my heart is still in a whirl.

Together we've seen our love unfurl
into such a beautiful thing.
How could we know what a precious pearl
the passing years would bring?

Life with you has brought such pleasure,
from the moment you said you were mine.
You will always be my greatest treasure,
my dearest, sweetest Valentine.

Don't call Me Granny

'Please don't call me Granny Dear'
I heard the woman say,
'It really is too much my dear
just run away and play.'

'I'm much too young to be
a Granny' she turned and said to me.
'Oh yes my dear I'm much too young
at only forty three.'

'The Children just don't understand
how important it can be,
to keep up appearances
when they come to visit me.'

'A sister or a brother
is what she really needs.
Someone who'll play ball and
search for daisies in the weeds

Someone who'll play hopscotch,
and roll upon the rug,
and maybe every now and then,
just give her a hug.

I haven't time for all these things,
I've far too much to do,
And if Granny's what she really needs
She should have somebody like you!

THE TIME MACHINE

I've just boarded my time machine,
though it's really a forty bus.
To visit the places I used to know,
when it used to be them, and us.

The place where all the water tanks
were put during the war.
In case Hitler scored a direct hit,
I've seen them all before.

The library just off Branch Road,
the Park, the School, the Pit,
The house where Lazy Daisy lived,
before her 'moonlight flit.'

Castleton school no longer stands,
no children to pass through her doors.
Armley jail took care of that,
the school that was mine and yours.

Come with me, I'll show you how,
it sprawls across the rubble.
The only ones who go there now,
are those who are in trouble.

I walked along to Armley Moor,
where the 'Welcome' used to be.
Remembering the fairground,
and folks like you and me.

Looking round me now I see
the new Karl Cohen Square,
While on the now dishevelled moor
horses are grazing there.

Wearily I climb back on the bus,
still remembering 'Them and Us.'
And happier times long gone before,
when you and I were only four!

Mail Order Mayhem

I've been dealing with Mail order
for more than forty years.
Now, it would seem after all this time
our association could end I fear.

'All our advisors are busy'
I'm constantly being told.
'Please hang up and try again'
or 'Would you like to hold?'

I am a busy woman
with lots of work to do,
My time is much too precious
to spend waiting in a queue.

Do you think they've been 'Taken Over?'
that would explain my fears.
They have been a Limited Company
for over a hundred years.

At last! I've placed my order,
and sent it in the Mail.
Sadly, that's just the beginning
of this sorry tale.

The garment has at last arrived
at my home, just yesterday.
Five weeks after ordering
I really have to say!

Now the problem is, returning it.
because it's not my size,
I still can't reach them on the 'phone
surely you've realised?

Now, I'll send the 'Return Form'
back to them by mail,
With a message to the 'Collection Van'
please call at my home again.

You'd think that in this modern age,
things would be much quicker.
That folks would polish up their act,
and really be much slicker.

Not everyone has access
to V. D. U.' s and C. D Rom.
And I really can't do business
with this w w. com.

When I Had You

The dawn still breaks
the sun still sets,
The skies are still as blue.
Yet everything has changed so much
since the days when I had you.

The moon still shines
the stars come out,
the grass still kissed with dew.
Yet everything has changed so much
since the days when I had you.

The seasons change
the rain still falls,
the world keeps turning too.
Yet nothing that is different
can change my love for you.

BEST FRIENDS

Daphne and I have always been friends,
ever since we were kids in school.
A couple of slum kids are what we were,
and being pals was the golden rule.

As children we always shared everything,
even our laughter and tears.
There were no TV's or computers to play,
yet our friendship has weathered the years.

When we grew up, to New Zealand she went,
far away over the sea.
That was when the letters began,
the scribbling between her and me.

When each of us wed, and our kids came along
we always had something to say.
Even if only to talk of the tricks,
that our children got up to each day.

Now we're retired, and she's back here to stay,
though it's just for a little while,
We've laughed and we've cried, and giggled and sighed,
though each parting has been with a smile.

Now the time has all gone and she's on her way home,
and it may be we'll not meet again.
Though perhaps if I try to New Zealand I'll fly,
when I find courage to get on that 'plane.

FIRST DAY AT SCHOOL

Where is the Little One I held in my arms?
nurtured and loved with Grandmotherly charms.
The babe that I cared for when Mum was at work,
never a duty, nor something to shirk.

Where's the toddler who went shopping with me?
knowing that Mum would be back at half three.
Who liked walking on walls, and watching the trains,
and kicking stray pebbles into the drains.

A real grown up four year old just phoned me to say,
"Grandma I'm starting at big school today!"
I can just see him now, in my mind's eye
saying to me proudly, "Gran, just look at my tie!"

ANOTHER SPRING

Once again the spring is here
the trees are not as green this year.
The skies above are not so blue,
nor the song birds notes as true,
Not the way they used to be
when you shared your life with me.

Newborn lambs don't seem to play
in their usual carefree way.
Or children while away the hours
in the fields now full of flowers.
That are not so bright to me
as when you shared your life with me.

Young lovers wandering hand in hand
haven't found that fairyland.
Where trees are green and skies are blue
and this old world again is new.
Just the way it used to be
when you shared your life with me.

Food For Thought

Unseen, unheard, silently watching
from a distant star.
Someone who knows exactly who,
and what we are.

Another planet, a different world,
waiting, like a rose unfurled,
For us to know that they are there,
whirling round the atmosphere.

For centuries we have always thought
what strange powers could be wrought?
if other planets that we were seeing,
were occupied by other beings

And is the universe a place, where
once conquered, we could travel there?
Could we cope with all the fuss
would there be room for all of us?

If there is life on Venus and on Mars.
maybe we can reach up to the stars.
And if tickets to the universe could be bought,
surely that would give us food for thought

IMPRESSIONS

Savage scenery, wild untamed.
water rushing, headlong.
Spluttering madly, careering.
into lochs and Burns.

Tall slender trees,
silhouettes scratching ever skyward.
Piercing the Heavens,
clutching at barren hillsides,
with curious searching roots.

Heather, blackened now
by winters frost.
Snow, clinging to hillsides
and boulders.
Wind, vicious, cutting, biting.
stifling sounds of birdsong
In its wake.

Hidden between perished grasses
snowdrops struggle to face the light.
Newborn lambs, snuggle
ever closer to the tired ewes fleece.

Now, a squirrel peers sleepily
from his drey.
A veil, a whisper of green,
begins to clothe the scratching branches.

Birds, busying with discarded feathers
twigs, and bits of wool.
Darting between sunbeams,
dodging scudding clouds that pass.

Ever joyful, the sun bestows
her kisses on the snow.
Gently now unlocks the grip
of winters vice.
Earth responds to nature
as before
And spring arrives again
in Aviemore.

ODE TO A DEAR FRIEND

I never contemplated losing you my Friend,
and that's what you were until the very end.

We used to share so many things.
our deepest thoughts and some silly things.
There's been a lot of laughter and some tears,
yet through it all we shared eleven happy years.
We knew each others secrets from the past,
our hopes for the future and the rest.
Your dearest wishes were not to be
but from where you are you will see,
Everything happen as it was meant to be.
that time was so short, we never guessed.
But ours was a friendship that was blessed,
sleep well old Pal, free from pain.
Perhaps one day we will meet again.

Do You Remember When

Do you remember when we lived
in the old mill yard?
When you and I were very young
and times were hard.

The fun we had, the games we played,
when we came home from school.
'Play in this yard, not up the street'
Dad said as a rule.

We had no choice but to obey
otherwise we could not play,
in this wonderland we'd found.
When we were young and times were hard,
and we used to live in the old mill yard.

Climbing on the rooftops
of the Weaving sheds,
We knew that it was dangerous
though we never lost our heads!

We'd run upon the coal stacks
in the engine house.
Searching for the crickets there,
and once we found a mouse

Our Mum, always busy, never ever knew,
the mischief we got into the way that children do.
In those days, when times were hard,
and we still lived in the old mill yard

We'd struggle over the bottom gate
on to the canal side,
Running over Oddy Locks
looking for somewhere to hide.

These were some of the "Good old days"
that we shared when were young.
We cannot bring them back again
the laughter and the fun.

But yet the memories will always be,
bright and fresh and new.
When we remember each sight and sound,
of those days when times were hard,
And we still lived in the old mill yard.

MY LEEDS

What makes the city of Leeds unique?
Is it the ordinary folk or just the business clique!
Could it be the parks and stately homes we share?
Even council houses, with children playing there.

Is it the entertainment and the nightlife in our city
Or are we northerners exceptionately witty?
All our mills and factories alas are gone,
a city of shopkeepers we have now become.

Could it be the Black Prince, who stands in City Square?
Maybe those football yobs creating havoc there!
Perhaps other teams have come along and sighted,
a vision of a Leeds now dis-united.

Maybe our Hospitals have done the trick?
though televising patients, does nowt to heal the sick!
A metropolis of accumulated wealth,
but sleepless nights don't do much to aid your health.

Is Leeds a city that never sleeps?
there's always action on our city streets!
No shortage of dance halls and clubs,
or even drug traffic in some of our pubs.

Yet we who live together side by side,
defend our town with immense pride.
Unique it is, I'm sure we've shown
just don't forget it is our home!

THE MILLENIUM

We stand on the threshold of another year
twenty-first century – almost here
What does the future hold in store?
rising prices, another war?

Unemployment, more space races
starvation and famine in far off places
Governments overthrown, kings exiled
is the whole world going wild?

Always taking rarely giving
disinclined to work for our living
"We're all right Jack, we won't fuss
Social security takes care of us"

We just can't go on this way,
struggling from day to day.
In this world of fear and doubt
everyone's taking the easy way out.

Are we so blind we cannot see
the rot in our society?
Work at our jobs as we do at play
do a fair days work for a fair days pay.

Raise our standards and our morals
then we shall have earned the laurels,
and prosperity we strive for
all those things brave men have died for.

Don't just say it isn't fair
get out and show the world you care,
Our future is what this is all about
act now for time is running out.

If's, But's And Maybe's

If I had been born to another life
would I have been a Mother?
Would I have been a wife?
Maybe I'd have been a beauty Queen
but what would I do then?
Maybe I'd have spent my life
surrounded by handsome men?

And maybe if I hadn't had
all the things I've had.
The dearest loving Mother
and the dearest Dad,
the kindest loving husband
a girl has ever known
and two loving Daughters,
that I'm proud to call my own.

But if my life had taken any other road,
then maybe I would have carried
a far, far heavier load
Yet after all is said and done
the if's and but's and maybe's gone,
The life I live is the life I've won
and I'm quite happy with it

THE PARSONAGE

I stood by the gates of the Parsonage
I heard the whispering in the trees,
I heard the voice of Cathy cry
to Heathcliffe on the breeze.
I never heard the soft reply
that rippled like foam on the seas.
I felt their despair as they parted
I knew the depth of their love,
leaving them both broken hearted
to wander the moors up above.
Now I am lost in their sadness
almost drowning in their despair,
needing someone to comfort me
hoping that someone will care,
And who knows, maybe these lovers
while haunting the moors that they love
may find the unspoken answers,
for all those who search for true love.

How Do You Know When You're Old?

How do you know when you're old?

When you're get up and go has got up and gone
you start to look back on all that you've done.
When you're back starts to ache
And you're blood's running cold.

How do you know when you're old?

You look back on your life
and the romance has gone,
You've never got used to living alone.
You remember the battles
you've lost and you've won.

How do you know when you're old?

When Your Grandchildren come,
they want you to play.
And you then have to sleep
For the rest of the day.

How do you know when you're old?

My reputation I don't want to sully,
but I shall grow old disgracefully.
Because now I m retired,
My life's just begun.

I'm going to go out and get me some fun,
I could live to be ninety before I'm done.
by then I shall know when I'm old!

Leeds -Then And Now!

Leeds is the centre of my being
it is the place where I lived and worked
all my life.
It is friendly, welcoming, modern
and very, very lively.

It has humour energy and compassion
Leeds is a green and pleasant place to be.
The slums where I was born and raised
have long since gone.

Modern buildings stand where once they stood ,
crumbled and decayed.
Leeds is the place my forbears chose to live and work
during the industrial revolution.

In my lifetime I have travelled to many towns and cities,
in some I have stayed for weeks at a time
in others I have lived for many months.
Leeds is the place I chose to put down my roots!

This is the place where I grew up,
where I met my man, and bore our children.
The one place where I would rather be, above any other.
What is it then that makes Leeds unique?
it is my HOME

WHEN YORKSHIRE MET FRANCE

We've bin on us 'olidays ter Foakston,
on't Wednesday we went ter Boulogne.
T'weather turned out reet gradely,
but what bother we 'ad with't coin,
They'd priced everythin' up i' them Euros,
and none of us could convert it back.
Do yer think they're all out ter diddle us
p'raps they've some knowledge we lack.

We kept goin' round l' circles,
ter get best price we could duty free.
But afore we got done we all 'ad ter run,
ter get back on't ferry yer see
I doan't mind visitin' them Frenchies
though I doan't understand what they say
I really doan't know 'ow I'd cope wi' 'em all
if I 'ad to be wi' 'em all day.

Letters To My Mum

Dear Mum
For all the times I spoke of you
as though you were not there,
when all the while you sat there
quietly in your chair.
I'm Sorry

For all the times
when I was sharp with you,
when your memory just would
not work for you.
I'm sorry

For all the times you asked
"Can we go home today?"
and I just didn't know
the right thing to say.
I'm so sorry!

Dear Mum,
For all the good times
that we shared,
the days when I knew how much
you really cared.
I'm glad

For all the laughter
and the happy hours,
the understanding
and companionship,
that was ours.
I'm glad

Now your hands are still,
your work is done.
There are no more battles to be won
I treasure the memory
of all that we had
and yet my dearest Mum.
I am so sad

LUCIFER

Who moves along with feline grace?
Who claims the chair by the fireplace?
Who eats and sleeps the whole day through?
Who always does what he wants to do?

Who often stays outside all night?
Who is the Victor in every fight?
Who catches mice and things like that?
Who else but Lucifer our cat!

Loose Chippings

I know a place, a quiet place
just meant for lovers meetings.
It's overheard some tender words,
some partings and some greetings.

It always has a moon and stars
some stars are even shooting.
It's only meant for two to share
though once a wise old owl was there.

It can be found on April nights
when all the trees are dripping.
The raindrops hang like fairy lights
in our Secret Place
Loose Chippings.

MY WINDOW ON THE WORLD

Each day I sit beside my window
on the world.
Observing life's miracle
as each new day unfurls.

The birds alert the morning some singing,
while in flight.
Welcoming each brand new day
as it emerges from the night.

The milkman's cheery whistle
as he rattles through the gate,
Postman close upon his heels,
although often he is late.

A District nurse calls 'most every day,
she tends the old lady across the way.
Daffodils nod a greeting to the sun,
on this new day that's just begun.

Carefree children with laughing faces,
some riding bikes, they're going places.
Others carrying their books, oh! what a weight,
hurrying along now, don't want to be late.

Reluctantly I turn to view my room inside.
moving very slowly to the cosy fireside.
Until tomorrow, when I shall sit and wait,
as the world and his Wife .pass my front gate

Only In Dreams

Only in dreams
our love has chance to live.
Only in dreams
that's all I have to give.

Lets leave the world outside
the hurt, the pain.
Come to my dreams each night
and hold me once again.

Only in dreams
I ache to hold you tight.
Only in dreams
I kiss your lips goodnight.

And when tomorrow comes
and dreams have flown.
I shall awake my love
to live my life alone.

POETRY

Whenever I feel tense or terse,
I get the urge to speak in verse.
Given chance to write it down
then I really go to town.

It's good to while away the hours,
writing verse on trees and flowers.
But when I only have a minute,
I write a poem with laughter in it.

When I am feeling sad or down
I try to stop and look around,
at those who suffer aches and pains
and try to cheer them up again.

The answer's really very simple
if you can produce a dimple,
and perhaps a smile or two
you'll find there's poetry in you.

PARTING

The aching void inside now that you've gone
hold up your head my love,
you said and carry on.
No more to meet in our own secret place
nevermore the warmth of your embrace.
I always knew one day I'd meet the one
who would be all my days,
my nights, my morning sun.
What had I done that fate should deal this blow
that taught me how to love and then to know,
the misery of a parting worse than death
that I'll remember 'til my dying breath.
I needed you my heart, to show to me
the wonder of the love you gave to me.

SLEEPLESS IN CROSSGATES

When I go to bed each night
and close my bedroom door,
I can't suppress the hatred
that I've felt so many times before.
The nights have robbed me of my sleep
hours and hours of counting sheep,
and aeroplanes that cross the skies
yet precious sleep evades my eyes.
I walk the floor while others slumber
finally into bed I clamber.
Sleepless still I find I'm shaking
and then I find the dawn is breaking

Seacroft Hospital

Sixty years ago, for just a short while,
this place was home to me.
It conjures up such memories
of how it used to be
Cleaners wearing Bright aprons,
with dusters and mops.

Iron bedsteads and wooden lockers
with bright shiny tops.
Matron and nurses all starched and white,
keeping their vigil through the long lonely night
Children crying in fever and pain,
unable to rest 'til it's daylight again.

Staff in the kitchen worked ten hours a day,
cooking for Patients, no time for delay.
When they were ready and pushed on to the ward,
the way they were welcomed,
was the staffs just reward.

The years have rolled on and I'm a patient still,
they care for the old, not just those who are ill.
Times have certainly changed since those days long ago
happily now. there's less sadness and woe.

Tommy Ticklethumb

Climb upon my knee, and listen to me,
we have time for a story just before tea.
Now I'll begin and if you are good,
I'll tell you about Johnny who lived in the wood.

A long time ago just between you and me,
a little old man came from over the sea.
He found his way over a mountain of sand,
into the palm of this little boys hand.

He had a quick smile and he laughed out with glee,
there was a wink and a wave for us all to see.
He loved to sing and to dance and to hum
this jolly old man our Tom Ticklethumb.

Johnny got up one morning and went out to play,
and very soon found that he'd lost his way.
He tried very hard to find his way home,
oh! How he wished that his Mummy would come.

Then, before he had time to say "Little Jack Homer"
his Mummy appeared from just round the corner.
He was so pleased to see her, he laughed out with glee,
"Oh, Mummy dear I just knew you'd find me."
She said "Come along Johnny lets go home for tea.

THE TREE

The music and the mystery of a tree
will always be a source of joy to me.
The tiny seed from whence it came
its branches reaching for the sun and rain.
Dressed in full green to greet the summer sun
now stark and bare ere wintertime's begun.
And when springtime comes around once more
those baby buds will burst just as before.
Four seasons now have passed – behold the tree
clothed once again in perfect majesty

The Great Exhibition

They're 'avin a great exhibition
dahn in't Armouries so they say.
An' they're wantin' ter show
all the work that we've done,
abah't what it were like in our day!

It wer in't days when nobody 'ad owt
never knew if we'd get any tea,
or even where't brass would come from
ter buy't next meal d'yer see?

We didn't get many pleasures, in them far off years
but we valued us friends an' us neighbours
and we shared i' there laughter an' tears.
But our lives must 'ave bin pretty special
if fowk want ter 'ear abaht em today!

The Quiet Times

The quiet time 'twixt dusk and dawn
that's the time I spend with you.
When sleep evades my eyes
and wakefulness comes smiling through.

It helps me to remember
those happy times we shared,
When you and I were oh, so close,
and I knew how much you cared.

Now you are in another place,
alas I cannot follow
It could be one day soon, perhaps.
who knows? maybe tomorrow.

Until that happy day arrives
there's much I have to do.
For no one else can make those
precious dreams we had, come true…

I do not mourn your passing
the way I did before,
In that quiet land I learned,
that death is but a door
that we must all pass through.
'Til that day comes,
not just in thought
I shall be there with you.

The Waterfall

Water, hurtling over rocks into a pool.
glistening, rippling, cascading joyfully
towards a bubbling stream.
Meandering through the countryside.
passing fields with grain and cattle.
Gurgling between the pebbles that lay close,
by buildings, and picturesque ruins.
Water, harsh and menacing,
grey clouds and thunderstorms.
Waves lashing the seashore.
crashing against harbour walls.

Lightning flashing, wind whipping
the sea into a crescendo of noise.
Now, a lagoon a haven of peace.
sunlight casting its' spell upon the water
peace, tranquillity and, finally
a lasting calm.

Fifty Years On

They told us all that this would be
a war to end all wars.
That ours would be the victory,
but we would bear the scars.

They never said that when we'd won the war
we would lose the peace,
that the fighting and the conflict
would never ever cease.

They could not know our world would be
in conflict still today,
will they never ever really see
that it's the ordinary folk who pay?

So many innocent children,
the old the weak the lame.
The mud the blood the hurt the pain
to suffer yet again.

Dear God, when will there be no more
when will this fighting cease?
Let's call an end to bloody war
then we can win the peace.

Rememberance Day

The soldier lies in Flanders field
muddied bloody and dead.
There he sleeps Eternally
at rest in his earthly bed.

Before the Cenotaph another stands
with bowed dishevelled head.
A wreath of poppies in his hands
his tribute to the gallant dead.

It worries not the warrior
that he's not well dressed nor smart.
It is enough that he remembers him
with a true and thankful heart.

To those who criticised this man
I have only this to say
'Twas his National pride
made him stand outside
to commemorate this day.

THE GREAT WAR

"What did you do in the Great War Daddy?"
"Me, I was in the eighth army then,
in charge of a battalion of men.
The D-day landings we fought our way through
Italy and North Africa too.
We left our homes, our children, and our wives
left behind our ordinary lives
to become soldiers who fought to the death"

"What did you see in the Great War Daddy?"
"I saw the misery of the holocaust
Belsen and Dachau were the worst.
So many families to count the cost
of the millions of lives so cruelly lost,
only to satisfy it would seem
the madness of a Dictators dream
who believed he would rule the world"

And what did you learn In the Great War Daddy?"
"I learned that greed and avarice create wars
born in great offices behind closed doors.
It is not the Ministers who die
nor their womenfolk who cry.
It's those of us in uniform
and our wives and mothers who are left to mourn,
while we fight on to victory!"

"What are your prayers for now Daddy?"
"My prayer is that we shall have world peace
that this lust for war will cease
and this senseless tyranny will be overcome.
Only then shall our heroes see
the profit in our victory
and our glorious dead at last will rest.

WORLD WAR TWO 1939 –1945

Do you remember when they said
"We've won the war"?
there were parties in the streets
and we all danced till dawn.
Yet there were those of us who stayed behind
to mourn, the husbands and the sons
who never would come home.
Who gave their lives for freedom, and the right
to roam this land we love so dear.

Do you remember when they said
that this has been a war to end all wars?
We shall have an everlasting peace
the fighting and the bloodshed has to cease.
We shall build the homes our heroes richly deserve,
a brave new start for those who served
and a monument to our gallant dead.

The reality is far from what we planned
there still is fighting out in Ireland
Rwanda Bosnia Rumania and the rest
"WORLD PEACE HAS NOT WITHSTOOD THE TEST"
When shall we see an end to bloody war
when bloodshed and massacres will be no more.
When this world is free from fear and hate
only then can we truly celebrate.

THE JUBILEE

When we were young, on 'Empire Day,'
there was a 'Coronation.'
For then we crowned 'Queen of the May,'
it was an annual celebration.
And then one day someone said,
'We must announce, the King is dead,
Long live the Queen!'

And that was how it came to pass,
the Nation took to this young Lass.
Elizabeth became Queen of the realm,
and she and Philip took the helm.
A whole year passed before the Nation
celebrated the Coronation in 1953.

Now fifty years have come and gone,
we've all seen many changes.
our young Queen's a Grandma now,
yet she still rules the nation.

So come on folks, lets raise a glass,
please join our celebration.
The toast is fifty golden years,
to us all and to the nation.
'God save the Queen!'

Summer Holidays

How the excitement is mounting
our cases all packed once again.
It's almost time for our holiday
and this year we're going to Spain.

Next Saturday we'll be off to the airport
our adventure's about to begin.
When we get up first thing in the morning
oh what a state I'll be in.

Alan is coming to fetch us
he's taking us round to their place.
There'll be Stan and me and our Adam
all three with big grins on our face.

We'll meet up with Matthew and Robert
and with their Mum, our daughter Elaine.
At last it's beginning to happen
we're off on our journey to Spain.

With car seat and potty and luggage to boot
we climb into the bus with all of this loot.
With all this excitement I don't feel quite sane
perhaps I'll calm down when I get on the 'plane.

Now it's on to the motorway the M62
as we're going to the airport this road will do.
We arrive at the airport there's so much to see
can you point out the shop where they sell
"duty free?"

The time has arrived and we're boarding the 'plane
all the excitement is mounting again.
We're taxiing along soon we'll be up, up and away
look out Spain we're coming your way.

Now it's three hours later how the time's flown
very soon now our 'plane will touch down.
We'll reach Alicante where our transport awaits
put our clocks back an hour don't want to be late.

At last we've arrived
we shall have so much fun.
At last our holiday as really begun

Our Daughter – The Bride

At last your wedding day is here
The day you've waited for
Your Dad and I have cared for you
With pride we've watched you grow
And now your special day is here
We wanted you to know
We wish you love and happiness
The best life has in store
Of all that you'll be wished today
No one could wish you more

THE YEAR OF 'FORTY-ONE

One night in Nineteen forty-one,
when the sirens began to wail,
We four hurried up Armley road
in the shadow of the Jail.

Mum, carried our little brother,
he was six months old.
A soldier took him from her,
And ran off with our precious load.

The bombs were falling thick and fast,
we could hear them as we ran.
Soldiers led us to the shelter,
And still the bombs continued their welter
on the railway, at the other side of the road.

At last we reached our destination,
Someone said !"Gerry's dropped one on the station
Maybe that's our quota for tonight"

When we got into the shelter,
it was quite cosy and warm.
At the far end there stood a Soldier,
With a bundle in his arms.

He wasn't much more than a teenager,
Embarassed by what he had done.
The child he had carried to safety
He gave back to my Mother, her son!

My Sister she was only four,
had chosen a spot by the shelter door.
I would have tried a similar trick,
But I was too busy being sick!

By the time we knew there was nothing to fear
we heard the sounds of the last "All clear"
Someone said "You can't go home.
At the end of your street they've dropped a bomb!

The Red Cross took us all to Mount Pisgah,
It's up Tong road, and not very far.
There were steaming cups of tea and coffee,
With biscuits you could n't break for toffee.

The very next day we were allowed to go home
To view the effects of a very large bomb!
It had dropped on the very first house in the street
An occasion we don't ever want to repeat.

All the windows were shattered,glass everywhere,
There was a terrible smell of gas in the air.
No water either, we couldn't make teas,
We are all going to end up evacuees.

"There's nothing else for it, it's too dangerous here
We're going to stay with your Aunt 'til next year."
We packed a few things and jumped on the tram,
Dad said "Our Edna will help us out of this jam."

It was a long time before we all went back home.,
I'm not sure that any one of us wanted to come
back, to the dirt and the dust and the soot.
That seemed to be every where that we set foot.

But in no time at all there was fresh bread on the plate,
And a really welcoming fire in the grate.
For the rest of the war no matter what Hitler tried,
We never again left our own fireside.

What am I

My given word means two things you see
The meanings of which are quite clear to me
One always appears on a music sheet,
And without it no song would be complete

Notes on a page, are music to the ear
Becoming a tune for all to hear
Sometimes they are played quite out of tune
Then the song is ended, often too soon.

Each one related to beats in a bar
The difference being how many there are.
Quavers and minims, semi- breve's, too,
All these are closely related to you.

While I relax and the music plays
I keep myself busy on most of the days.
I sit with the yarn. and my fingers, fly
How very quickly the hours pass by.

Bedspreads, blankets, cushion covers too,
All of these are born of you
It's all down to your fashion and also your style
That my hobby as always, is so worthwhile

So what is my word have any of you guessed
Or are you still pondering, trying your best
I will not give in I can hear you say
Surely you've realised the word is crotchet

FRAGMENTS

Time, like grains of sand
Filtering down into the universe.
Snatches of an old song,
Tantalising the memory.

Forever yours, at the end of a letter
Betrayal, and the ensuing heartache.
A splinter of conversation
From a teenage friendship,

Followed by that first kiss
From the boy next door.
One half of a photograph
Severed at the end of an affair,

Tears of bitterness and pain.
Faded flowers pressed in a book,
A wedding bouquet.
Baby's first tooth, a teenage student.
University degree.
One half of a couple – Fidelity!

All these are fragments of a whole,
One being, one entity
Living life to the full,
From now to Eternity.

TO MY BROTHER AND HIS WIFE

A precious little infant has
Made all your dreams come true.
Your very first granddaughter,
how wonderful for you.

Heaven sent this little one
To make your lives complete
A dearer, sweeter infant
you couldn't wish to meet.

Now that you are Grandparents
a duty you must share
New babies I am sure you know
need lots of love and care.

At last you have a grandchild,
of your very own.
Hope you share the happiness
that other folks have known.

Teach her all the little things
you learned at Mothers knee.
Enjoy lots of hugs and kisses,
every time she comes to tea.

Make sure that she has lots of space,
when it's time to play.
Pretend games will be different,
every time she comes to stay.

Expect the unexpected
it's the only thing to do.
She will be sure to let you know,
she thinks the world of you.
That will also be the time,
she knows you love her too.

THE CATHEDRAL

Its magnificent beauty,
Thrusts toward the heavens.
Piercing the skies in its search
For infinity and truth.
Exploring the atmosphere,
Transmitting the power of the universe
To all those who seek to believe.
It was fashioned and carved by men
With both vision and belief.
A perfect legacy that tells
Its pilgrims of the glory
That is Wells.

P. C. Pain

I have a new computer,
I like it very much.
But when it comes to inspiration,
I fear I've lost my touch.

I sit at my work station,
And though it's not my aim
I guess that I'm just wasting time,
Playing computer games.

Perhaps when inspiration comes,
Like a bolt out of the blue.
Then maybe I shall turn out work
As expertly as you!

AFTERMATH

I never thought there'd be a time
When I could say these words to you.
That you were right and I was wrong,
And love would see us through.

I truly thought that when you died,
My life had ended too.
I needed strength to carry on,
Oh how I needed you.

You were my one and only love
No longer by my side
Two long years have come and gone
And I can say with pride
You must have seen this strength in me
When I became your bride.

Now at last the time has come
To leave you in the past.
In that special place you'll be
Amongst my fondest memories
The ones that are made to last

A Gift For Christmas

Christmas time is here once more
And it's time to trim the tree.
A time for us all to celebrate
Not just you and me!

I've bought some festive wrapping
To put my present in
But try as I might it just wasn't right
The blooming thing wouldn't fit in

I've struggled and struggled, far into the night
But somehow or other I can't get it right,
It bulges in the middle and the corners won't fit
I'm sure there's a grin in the middle of it.

I've stuck and I've pleated and folded,
Done my best to make it look neat
Then as soon as I think I've got the job done
A giggle falls out at my feet.

The gift that I give is meant for all
One that will be remembered long after
By the rich and the poor the young and the old
The most precious gift of laughter

FULL OF YOU

It's many years since last we met,
Yet I am full of you.
The way you'd always hesitate,
When I walked up to you.
Of how you would incline your head,
To hear each single word I said.
Just to be sure you understood,
Exactly as I knew you would.

So many years we've been apart,
Yet I am full of you.
You're with me as each day begins,
And at its' closing too.
I hold you close within my heart,
You're part of all I do.
This way I'm never lonely,
Just so full of you

Parting

The aching void inside now that you've gone,
hold up your head my love, you said and carry on.
No more to meet in our own secret place
nevermore the warmth of your embrace.
I always knew one day I'd meet the one
who would be all my days, my nights, my morning sun.

What had I done that fate should deal this blow,
that taught me how to love and then to know
the misery of a parting worse than death.
That I'll remember 'til my dying breath
I needed you my heart, to show to me,
the wonder of the love you gave to me.

Growing Up

I went out to the garage
just the other day.
And stood amongst the toys and things
where my grandsons used to play.

Hanging there upon the wall
was Adams old go-cart.
The toy that he loved most of all
bless his little heart.

Right next door to this was
Roberts' shiny scooter.
He used to ride into the street
blowing on its hooter.

Just one look and you can see
Matthews bike stood by the wall.
It's not much use today though
the frame is far too small.

Looking at the calendar
that hangs upon the wall,
I realise that we've moved on
the boys are grown so tall.

Now the theme is football
the Boro' and Man United
The question that I ask myself
'Why do they get so excited'

Then Mathew will come along
and pop his head around the door,
'Do you still make Granny buns
the way you did before?'

My life is so much slower now
until our Adam calls to say,
'Hello Grandymoo,
and how are you today?'

WINTERS WONDERLAND

Stars hang suspended in a dark blue night,
winter frost paints the countryside white.
Bright cozy fires set the hearth aglow,
Christmas with holly and mistletoe.

Cloud soft snow falling through the trees,
swept up in drifts at the slightest breeze.
Gas lamps shedding their golden glow,
on virgin white in the street below.

Carriage wheels muffled in snow white streets,
ice covered lakes spread silvery sheets.
A waterfall held in winters vice,
natures symphony in ice.

Large round snowmen in bowler hats,
warm friendly houses with welcome mats.
Lanterns flicker whilst carolers sing,
away in the distance church bells ring.

The message is changeless from year to year,
lift up your hearts and be of good cheer.
We hear the old greeting again and again,
peace be upon the earth, Good will to men.

LONELINESS

Picture a vast, wide open space.
A bare and barren empty place
that stretches as far as the eye can see,
this is what loneliness means to me.

Often I'm in crowded places
filled with many different faces.
Each reaching out for their own kind
complete togetherness of heart and mind.

Picture now a lonely soul
hoping one day to be whole.
Seeking someone just like me
with whom to share eternity.

THAT SPECIAL PERSON

My friend I think you are afraid,
you hold out your hand and give the needy aid.
Yet you do not want them to depend
or to rely too much on you my friend.
You say that you are just an ordinary bloke
yet you hold the power to evoke,
in other minds such confidence in you
giving your strength to help the other through.
It seems to me you are a man who cares
very much about the way the other fellow fares.
The challenge is to see his problem now resolved
and suddenly you find yourself involved.
Now you have met a mind just like your own
a rich reward for all the seeds you've sown.
Someone who thinks and reasons as you do
another soul who fills the need in you.

Spring.

The earth is waking from its wintry bed
there is a fresh crisp cleanness in the air.
And spring rejoices as we tread the paths
where primroses and snowdrops grow,
and swiftly following on, the bluebells
soon will show, their pretty heads.
Welcoming each brand new day
and nodding gaily as we pass.

RICHES

The joy in your heart on a bright spring morn
the sun coming out to welcome the dawn.
Green grassy slopes a bird flying high
these are the things that money can't buy.

The fragrance of a summer breeze
flower filled hedgerows tall graceful trees.
The magic in a starlit sky
these are the things that money can't buy.

The fragrance of flowers long after they're gone
remembered lines from a lovely old song.
Laughing children a babies first cry
all these are the things that money can't buy.

EILEEN

If you met my friend Eileen,
you'd know her right away.
She has a love of animals
that grows from day to day.
Dogs and cats and squirrels too,
come calling at her door,
Lots of them have been there
many times before.
She feeds them all on beef and nuts,
chicken and all the rest.
For her beloved animals,
it's nothing but the best.
And when the winter evenings come,
and it's cold and wet outside.
Then Eileen and her animals,
are snug and warm inside.

Travelling Companions

You asked if I would go away with you,
and I think of the places you would take me to.
China, Morrocco ,Greece and Rome
without a thought of coming home.

All my questions you could answer,
if we ever got the chance to
see the things that interest us
with the minimum of fuss.
Mosques, museums temples and places
which to me just now are faceless.

Not for reasons of emotion
would you take me o'er the ocean.
I think that you misunderstood,
the reasons why I said I would.
The answers simple it's because
without you now would be my loss.

THOUGHTS

What do other people do,
with thoughts that overflow their minds?
Do they set them down as I do
or do they merely draw the blinds,
shutting out the overflow
giving them no chance to grow.
Or do they view them in the light of day,
and learn what they have tried to say.
Do they try to figure out
what life is really all about?

BROTHER

A warm and gentle giant of a man
firm but gentle, not the sort to inflict harm.
He'd travelled far and lived abroad,
but did not turn his back upon those who cared.

When the illness came he did not complain,
fought back with dignity and carried on the same.
It was too late to save him, that we all knew,
he did not deserve the pain that he went through.

And when at last he reached the end,
it was so hard to say goodbye to him,
He was my friend,
my confidante, my Brother

1st October 1940 – 31st January 2005

ETHICS 2001

I am alone, I am bereft,
a tiny soul upon a table left.
Leaving my family,
with broken hearts.
I am a commodity,
labelled 'Spare Parts.'
No matter what Society may say
I am the carnage that is Alder Hey.
Perhaps my family
would have been more at ease,
with the courtesy of
a simple' PLEASE'!

CONVERSATION

There is an air of sanity
about the world when you're with me,
and time appears of no account
at least it never does amount
to anything, when you are there.
We have so much to say and share
it passes by on silent wings,
while we're discussing other things
that most folks find uninteresting.

We shall not put the world to rights
in maybe half a dozen nights.
Yet in our minds we can create
a world that's free from fear and hate,
that we may enter hand in hand
a place that can be wonderland.
Filled with wonder and elation,
because we had our conversation.

THE ONE ARMED BANDIT

My love has a friend who's a Bandit,
square chested with one arm of iron.
His diet is pieces of silver and
his figure you must keep an eye on.

Sometimes he won't part with a shilling,
at others generous to a fault.
You should hear the roar, how the men shout
when he spits the jackpot out.

Quite often they spend hours together,
my Love and this tight fisted sinner.
But one of these days come foul or fair weather,
my Love will be the outright winner

OUR DAUGHTER-B.A.

The great hall is full,
the doors open wide.
So many dignified people inside.
The Chancellor is here,
Her Royal Highness too.
But, most important of all there is you.
You have worked long and hard
That's clear to see,
and we are so very proud
that you have got your degree.

The Author of this anthology was born and bred in Leeds. She was educated at Armley Park Secondary School in the forties.

In the fifties she met and married her late husband Stanley Mason. She has two Daughters and three Grandsons.

Although she left school with no formal qualifications at the age of fifteen, she has always had a keen interest in writing, and has had several of her poems published in various magazines and anthologies, an achievement of which she is justifiably proud.

Printed in the United Kingdom
by Lightning Source UK Ltd.
130992UK00002B/262-333/P